UNLEASHED

UNLEASHED
The Wit and Wisdom of Calvin the Dog

CALVIN T. DOG

Translated by Chris Glaser
Illustrated by Jim Kelley

Westminster John Knox Press
Louisville, Kentucky

Book design by Jennifer K. Cox
Cover design by Jim Kelley

First edition
Published by Westminster John Knox Press
Louisville, Kentucky

This book is printed on acid-free paper that meets the
American National Standards Institute Z39.48 standard. ♾

PRINTED IN THE UNITED STATES OF AMERICA
98 99 00 01 02 03 04 05 06 07 — 10 9 8 7 6 5 4 3 2 1

Library of Congress Cataloging-in-Publication Data

Glaser, Chris.
    Unleashed : the wit and wisdom of Calvin the dog / Calvin T. Dog ;
translated by Chris Glaser.
        p.   cm.
    ISBN 0-664-22116-5
    1. Dogs—Humor.   I. Title.
PN6231.D68G58   1998
818'.5407—dc21   97-47377

To all the homeless philosophers
in shelters throughout the world

Contents

The Wit and Wisdom of Calvin the Dog

The Way of Jesus in a Culture like Ours

Introduction:
Why Me?

So many of you like to guess what dogs are thinking as we sit pensively beside you that I've decided to play turnabout, and guess what you, the reader, must be thinking. How can a dog, humble in nature, a mixed breed of uncertain heritage, adopted from the Humane Society, who has experienced the world largely through the front window of a home in Atlanta—how can such a dog offer a philosophy of life that might have universal applications? Surely this must be what you're wondering. And *my*, you're *so cute* as you ponder it!

This book is my reply to your unspoken question about what we dogs think but have difficulty communicating. At least, this will tell you what *I'm* thinking. If you take the trouble to learn our language, you will discover for yourself what we try to tell you by our looks, licks, sniffs, nudges, bites, barks, scratches, jumps, and postures as well as our chewing, resisting, playing, stretching, and curling

at your feet, on your bed, next to you or *on* you—lap or otherwise.

I need to qualify the leavings that follow. What I've sniffed out—that is, my philosophy—is fed and watered as well as leashed (that is, limited) by my *Sitz im Leben*—that's German Shepherd for "situation in life." Thus I must describe myself and my lifestyle so you know through what olfactory membranes, as it were, I experience the world.

I have physical characteristics marked by my mixture of three breeds: golden retriever, labrador, and chow. Objectively, the mix makes my face endearingly cute to humans (though I'd rather think myself handsome), making them want to pat me on the head or hug me round the neck.

My body is big and as strong as it needs to be, but perhaps a little big for my head (or vice versa, my head is a tad too small for my body)—causing weight-conscious humans to displace their own fat anxiety onto me. The largeness of my body is both a blessing and a curse: a blessing when it comes to protecting my turf and my pack; a curse when it frightens human puppies whose faces I love to lick and cats whom I love to sniff. My fur is a beautiful golden-yellow brown, soft to the touch.

I tell you this not to elicit contact from the inevitable pet groupies among you who would delight to have me in your lives, but rather to say that, because of my looks, I enjoy somewhat of an advantage over less seemly dogs. It was my winsome appearance that gave me the edge over my siblings at the shelter, where I was chosen for adoption first over my plainer brown and grey brother and sister puppies. (What helped me endure my separation from those other furry bundles of warmth, safety, and play was that I slept throughout the entire transaction.)

Yet I have come to learn that my mixed breeding makes me less desirable to many humans who mistakenly believe that purebred creatures are superior. I suppose it's "natural" in a mechanistic society moving toward greater and greater specialization to suppose that animals bred for certain duties or traits are more valuable than those of us with mixed natures and behaviors. But in a *humane* society, I believe that we would *also* be prized—partly *because* of our uniqueness. In such a world, worth is not based on function, and diversity is valued—not something to be barked at, quarantined, or overtrained.

I was, at first, protected from the knowledge of mixed-breed prejudice by the humans who adopted me, adored me as if I had been born to them, and couldn't have loved me more if they had paid $300 to have me. It's from other humans that I learned my kind is less desirable, from the one who first disparagingly called me "mutt" to those who pointed out the black spots on my tongue, indicating my chow heritage, of which, incidentally, I have become fiercely proud.

I have a comfortable den with humans who treat me extraordinarily well. This has elicited my naturally sanguine and friendly nature. We are not rich, except in love. They feed me food that is healthy, keep my water bowl filled, bestow me with occasional treats, bathe me every few weeks, give me regular checkups at the vet's, vaccinate me annually, and dispense my monthly heartworm and flea medicine. I enjoy the run of the house and yard and sleep with them in their king-size lair at night. Almost daily, one of them takes me to a nearby park for a chance to roam free of all those restraints which humans—however well-intentioned—feel are necessary for dogs. Every other day, I'm taken for a walk in the neighborhood—leashed, but free to set my own agenda when it comes to savoring earthy aromas and making my own marks on the world.

I suspect that this description of my circumstances will cause the more politically correct in the canine world to snarl with anger and disgust, believing that such care is the height of paternalism, an echo of our colonialization by imperialistic humans. *Man's best friend, indeed*, they would growl. And though I sometimes flash back to the call of the wild, I am quickly sobered by the reality that a dog's life is, for the most part, easier than a wild animal's—or even a human's, for that matter. I'll comment more about this later.

One of my humans' caring acts leaves me with mixed feelings, and may make you question my ability to serve as a lead dog for others: I have been neutered. This does not mean that I do not have sexuality, nor does it mean I am incapable of intimate relationships. It does, however, limit still further my run of the world, as I can neither sow wild oats nor sire puppies. But my humans have assured me that, historically, eunuchs have been entrusted with great affairs of state as members of royal courts. They were defended by such prominent human religious figures as Isaiah and Jesus. And, my humans like to point out, celibacy has been considered by many religions to be a gift that allows a creature greater intimacy with God and with fellow creatures, as well as much-needed perspective on the canine—er, human—condition. So that is how I choose to view my imposed celibacy—as an opportunity rather than an obstacle.

Were it not for the overall good care I receive from my humans, I would not have been able to develop my philosophy or write this book. Certainly the attentiveness of one of my humans makes possible this translation. That human—who has a degree in theology—has taught me some human philosophy. And

I've devoured a few books of philosophy on my own. I found them to be rather dry, and not half so tasty as the Persian rug. Beauty wins out over truth once more.

I finally must point out that because I'm somewhat privileged as dogs go, my philosophy may not
adequately take into account the plight of my sisters
and brothers who are less fortunate in terms of nature and nurture. Though my personal experience is
limited, I do have indirect experience from other
dogs I've encountered on walks, who are either running dangerously loose in the streets or are separated from one another by walls and fences and
leashes. I listen to the wailing and whining of dogs
nearby who are maltreated or underfed. I also witness dogs out in the world through the window-
that-constantly-changes.* From these sources, I
have gnawed out the marrow of life from the experience of those less and more fortunate than I am,
and am thus better able to sniff out truth and meaning, goals of any philosophy.

I called this introduction *Why Me?* It's my personal version of a modern phrase, "the scandal of
particularity," that I've been told some human the-
ologians use to describe specific revelations of God's
work in the world, to some a scandal that the sacred

---

* This is the literal meaning of the Canine word for televi-
sion. —Trans.

within and behind all things surfaces in particular places, times, or beings. I am not so bold as to claim that my philosophy is a revelation of God in the world. Yet I do believe that a keen sense of hearing allows one to hear God's still small voice in every place.

And I believe that the scent of the Creator, or the sacred impulse, is in every creature. The human mystic Meister Eckhart said that even a caterpillar is so full of God a sermon* would prove unnecessary. Anyone who's tasted a caterpillar knows exactly

---

* I've left this word as Meister Eckhart used it, but there is no Canine equivalent for *sermon* alone—the idiom for *good sermon* is *barking-up-the-right-tree* and for *bad sermon* is *barking-up-the-wrong-tree.* —Trans.

what he means. We all reveal the holy as particular creatures, given our nature and our nurture. Forgive me, but I think it's a little arrogant for humans to think they're the only ones made in the image of God! I believe *every* creature is a locus for divinity.

I have described my particularity in this introduction. Out of unique creatureliness and experience, I offer my philosophy which, in turn, may curl up with your own. The whole truth of life is more than any one dog can chew, and I have a bone to pick with any canine or human philosopher or theologian who might claim to have digested everything. We each regurgitate what we cannot digest. We each have a bite of ultimate truth, a taste of life's purpose, and a scent of the sacred.

It is as a pack that we travel in spiritual quest. That's why it's vital that we share whatever insightful morsels and delightful treats we discover along the way. That's why I offer mine in this modest volume. My hope is that in doing so I may serve as a lead dog for other creatures—not just dogs and humans—to engage in the barking that guides us all on the run that is life.

Calvin
Atlanta, Georgia

On Collars

Humans may feel that wearing a dog's collar would be degrading. But, when you consider that it's the only article of clothing that we are usually required to wear, dogs are better off than humans. Every morning as I watch my humans put their clothes on, I thank God that I was born with my equivalent already in place. I don't have to worry about dressing or laundering or dry cleaning. (I know about dry cleaning because I've accompanied my humans to the dry cleaners.) Nor do I have to be concerned about fashion. Especially now that fur on humans is unfashionable, I proudly show off my lustrous golden coat, never having to worry about an animal rights activist (Bless their souls!) throwing paint on it.

When I was a puppy, I wondered in wide-eyed amazement that humans had to put their "skins" on, until I realized the nature of clothes, which I then came to believe was a kind of fur-envy. But, being advantaged as I was, I soon looked less judg-mentally and more benevolently on their need for dress. Humans—I came to think—are *so dear* in their desire to be like us, covering their bare skins. Yet they're never quite sure what breed they want to be, so each day, and sometimes more than once a day, they change coats.

As I said earlier, humans might think of dog collars as degrading. But here again, they show their wish to be more like us. Just as our collars usually reveal our identities and to whom we be-long, so, too, humans differentiate their identities and their packs by the collars they wear. For ex-ample, there are blue collars and white collars. Members of each of these groupings demonstrate appropriate pride in their pack, but sometimes their pride borders on arrogance as they judge themselves better than those wearing a different color collar.

Those people who are said to be reconcilers among all human breeds and mediators between hu-mans and God wear clerical collars. Yet, for what I think are obvious reasons, they also may take too much pride in their pack, or at least in themselves as individuals. I say "obvious" because *all* who consider

themselves called to play such a pivotal role in human and divine affairs must necessarily have a higher view of themselves than they probably ought to have.

One of my humans likes to quote Isak Dinesen, a human writer who defined pride based on observing animals in their natural state. In her book *Out of Africa*, she wrote: "Pride is faith in the idea that God had, when [God] made us. . . . Love the pride of God beyond all things, and the pride of your neighbor as your own."*

Animals respect one another's pride. We do not demand that a zebra behave like a lion, or a cat behave like a dog. We also do not demand that every dog behave like every other dog. We anticipate each creature to be true to itself. This doesn't mean that old dogs can't learn new tricks, as humans like to say; that is, we're not limited only to so-called "natural" means of expression. Nor does it give excuse for gratuitous violence against others; after all, nature's way embraces violence only out of a need for survival. Being true to ourselves means simply that

* Isak Dinesen, *Out of Africa* (New York: Vintage International Edition/Random House, 1989) 150–51.

our natures are sacred—no matter how different we are from one another—and that finally all packs, all prides, are God's.

So collars are important, but not ultimately so. They temporarily identify us and to whom we belong. Yet eternally and essentially we belong to our Creator.

On Barking

For the most part, dogs bark to defend our turf.
Before I actually learned to bark myself, I learned
this fact as a puppy. My humans and I would pass a
yard or house and a dog would bark angrily, letting
us know that we'd better stay away. Now, as an
adult, I do the same. But I'm learning to tell the difference between those who might be a real danger
and those who are not. Mail carriers and delivery
persons, for instance, pose no threat. Neither do the
cats that sometimes sit on our porch swing in front
of my window and under my nose, but sometimes I
just bark at them anyway. Other dogs, of course,
need to know that our front yard is mine. But
friends coming to visit—canine or human—may
even play with me.

I've noticed that humans bark too, and it seems
to be for the same reason: to protect their turf.
Some human barking is very loud and shrill. They
call each other bad names regarding their species,

gender, religion, and sexuality. They have a saying about sticks and stones breaking their bones, but names never hurting them—but I'm not so sure. When I bark, I feel a surge of fear and anger mixed with madness; it leaves me tired and drained. When others bark at me, I am surprised and scared and sometimes ashamed (like when I get barked at for emptying the wastebaskets). So I think barking hurts those on both sides of the fence.

But most human barking is so subtle and genteel it sounds respectable. On the window-that-constantly-changes I witness humans barking about immigration, borders, language, race, class, and status. Often, it seems to me, they haven't yet learned to tell the difference between what is a real threat and what is not. With all the unnecessary barking, I tune them out like I would the proverbial wolf who cried "Boy!" one too many times.

A documentary on my kind said that dogs bark rarely in the wild, but often in captivity. I wonder if that's why humans bark so often. The bark may be a desperate cry for freedom in the midst of their domestication.* As for me, I'm learning to bark only when absolutely necessary. I suggest others do the same.

---

* Canine equivalent of *civilization*. —Trans.

On Evolution

Recently a scientific report claimed "definitively" that we dogs are descended from wolves. Now, I'm quite willing to believe that humans evolved from apes, because they act like apes much of the time (I've been outside a singles bar). But I refuse to believe that I evolved from such a wild creature as a wolf—I'm much too refined for that.

Rather, I believe that I and other dogs were created by God and made in God's image. We are God's mirror reflection. That's why *God* backwards spells *dog*. Isn't that one of the first things you English-speaking humans notice, the spelling thing? And who else but God loves as unconditionally as a dog? We don't care who you humans are or what you humans do, as long as you take some time to be with us, praise us, worship us, and do our bidding occasionally. Isn't that godlike? Even when you treat us badly or forget we're around, the minute you turn about and give us the attention we deserve, we lick your faces and give you comfort. Isn't that divine?

On
Attentiveness

In a special training class at the pet store, my humans learned about "attentiveness." They were told to train me to be attentive to their wishes. But attentiveness has to be mutual for any relationship to work. They have had to learn how to be attentive to my needs as well: when I need to go out, when I need water or food, when I need to play, when I need to be petted, even when I need boundaries set for me—like being forbidden to chase a squirrel across the street.

They have learned to "read" me, though they are still not fluent in the Canine language. (My human who is translating this has had to look up almost every other bark or gesture of mine in the Canine-English dictionary he found in a mysterious little antiquities shop in Bristol, England.) Reading me is a way of understanding without a need for words, like an old couple who have been together a long time, speak little, but know what each other is thinking or feeling by the smallest gesture, the slightest change of demeanor or body language, the tone of voice in the simplest comments.

In the same way, I have learned to read my humans: when they want to be left alone, when they might take me for a walk, when they are sad or depressed, when they need me to climb on them to lick their faces. Words are only one form of communication. To truly love someone means being attentive to what's going on without always waiting to hear them bark.

This maxim applies to things as well. To truly love some*thing* means being attentive to an object without being asked. Things don't talk, anyway. For instance, if either of my humans' cars needs attention, Chrysler and Mazda can't say it in words. They speak in rattles or how much gas they eat or whether they can move. If humans pay attention, they can take better care of the things of this world.

Dog biscuits don't talk either, but there's a wonderful Zen meditation on sniffing and eating a dog biscuit that indirectly gives it voice, describing its history as a plant transformed by sun and water and soil to grain, harvested by a farmworker, ground by a grinder, baked by a baker, boxed by a packer, transported by a trucker, stacked by the pet store worker, and brought home by your human—all with care, and all for the taste sensation that is the dog biscuit's ultimate sacrifice. It seems to me that being attentive to all that goes into such things as dog biscuits would induce more human gratitude and expand human pleasure.

The holy doesn't always bark or grab us with its mouth either, but speaks through others, through things and events. To hear the sacred requires special attentiveness, listening regularly and intentionally for inspiration. Mystics are like half of that old couple I just mentioned, who, with very little stimuli, may hear or see or smell or taste or feel God or their Higher Power even in minutiae.

Sometimes people experience God in tragedy, saying things like, "This must be God's will." But I believe that, like a mother dog, God doesn't want us to get hit by cars, develop distemper or worms, or suffer abuse. I do believe, however, that in sad things I may hear God whimpering to be careful and care for myself and others, and feel God licking wounds as needed. God, I believe, is also attentive to us, feeding the birds that do not store food for themselves and knowing even the sparrows that fall to the ground, as the mystic Jesus said.

Mutual attentiveness is the spiritual gravity that holds all packs together, whether that of our families or that of our galaxy, as, like planets and stars, we whirl around one another, knowing we need one another's hold to prevent any of us from flying off alone as strays.

On Going to Church

I love going to church. I enjoy exploring the cavernous building filled with so many rooms, slipping on the shiny tiles, and I take pleasure running around outside in the yards surrounding the church, sniffing the scents of so many other animals.

But I do not sense why it's something my humans want to do, for they are made to sit and stay in but one room of the building on hard sofas for an hour or more while one person barks, allowed occasionally to stand and bay together at the yowl caused by someone scratching the teeth of a box. The best part of that time is when they walk around and pet each other, passing the treat of God. Their only other reward for being good through all this is hot muddy water and, occasionally, treats.

How can they feel wonder at God when they are kept in a box like this? They can't even look out the opaque windows of the church to view the graceful old trees and lawns around it. Surely they'd feel more gratitude toward God if they were outside in natural beauty! Certainly running and leaping and playing would fill them with greater ecstasy than being told to "sit" or "stand." Just feeling free to explore other God-boxes would be more exciting!

I still like going to church, just for different reasons than my humans.

On Ancestors
and Siblings

Humans look too much to biology to define their ancestors and family. I never knew my father, and I was separated from my mother and siblings once I was weaned. I consider my ancestors to be those dogs who came before me in my human family, and my family are my humans and those dogs I meet now.

One of my humans had a wonderful dog named Cindy as a child, who taught the youth what it meant to care for and enjoy a dog. Cindy made it possible for my human to love all dogs, and to want a house with a yard partly to adopt a dog. A huge portrait of Cindy hangs on the wall of our staircase. My immediate predecessor in this human's life was Sly, who has since retired and moved to Palm Springs.

My other human grew up with a dog that bit the poor thing regularly, apparently for no reason, though I daresay the dog, named Freckles, must have been abused by children my human's size.

Those who have been bitten often bite others, you know. But this human began the conversion toward appreciating dogs when living with a dog named Smokey in college. Smokey would drop a ball in my human's lap in the midst of studying or working on papers, an important reminder to take time to play. I am very grateful to my ancestor Smokey, because he made my human more agreeable to adopting another retriever mix—me—and my human is now fully converted as a "dog person"—even to the point of translating this book.

Just as these ancestors whom I never knew nonetheless have touched my life, so the dogs I meet today also have an effect on me, and I consider them my brothers and sisters. Riley was my first good buddy, and he would come and play with me on his walks with one or the other of his humans. But Riley had a wild side. One day, he and I just took off into the ravine behind the house, and our humans watched helplessly as we disappeared into the kudzu jungle.

I admired Riley's independence, and his charisma lured me into doing something I'd always wanted to do but didn't have the nerve to do by myself. We had quite a little adventure together before we became separated—and I became lost. Within an hour, with great glee on both sides, I was found by my humans, whom I had greatly distressed.

Riley was found that time, too, but he has since disappeared. Reward signs were posted by his humans, who offered a $500 reward! That translates into a lifetime of treats! Perhaps Riley was too independent for his own good, living the fast life running the ravine. I've wondered if he met an untimely end, or if some other human found him and has given him a new den. I miss him terribly. Whenever he came near our house, I would whine and jump around, begging my humans to let me out to play with him. Now, he never comes, though I keep watch.

Schultze, a beagle, lives with the mother of one of my humans in California, and I consider him an older cousin, though we've never met, except by scent carried by his human and my humans from Los Angeles. Our correspondence is what gave me the inspiration for writing this book. I also have a cousin, Mandy, who has a bad reputation for mischievousness. She lives with two aunts of one of my humans in Oklahoma. So far, she's chewed shoes, needles, and a set of false teeth!

I meet other dogs on my walks. Like Riley, Buster also manages to break out of his backyard, but he's old enough—and wise enough—to find his way home again. He's lively when he's free. But when he's inside the fence, his tired old bones may or may not rise to the occasion of greeting me at his gate. Black-and-white Oreo apparently never gets out. His yard is pretty secure. He lunges at us in a friendly way, but his play is frustrated by the fence.

Brown-haired Butch lives in a house with no fence, so when he's outside he runs free a lot of the time, buddying up with a nameless younger white-haired dog who seems to be his sidekick. Two pairs of bullying dogs live on either side of the street close to the park. They've never introduced themselves; they just bark like crazy when we pass. They are mean—or at least defensive—brothers and sisters, but still siblings. And finally, Kensey lives across the street from our house, a gentle, black pit bull who nonetheless defends his turf.

That reminds me to say that other dogs are not my only siblings. Kensey has a human named Wilson who's but two years old (fourteen in dog years), and I love licking his face while he giggles. Small humans and dogs have a lot in common. We are either treated well or badly by big humans. So I consider Wilson a sibling. Providentially for us all, our humans treat us well. A nearby neighbor ignores her dogs, and to me it's a wonder that she's involved in a custody battle for her human child.

I have a sister that other dogs in their bigotry might shame me for: a cat, a calico cat. There used to be laws in my home state of Georgia that forbad fraternization between a dog and a cat, I believe. The taboo is still strong, but we have, from the start, run up to one another and sniffed each other's forbidden scent. On my walks, we seek each other out.

Finally, some of my "family" are total strangers, like Grace, whom we found lost in the park. The resemblance between us was uncanny, though she was smaller and more fine-featured. We took her back to her home in Cabbage Town, a poor section of Atlanta nicknamed from the days it was populated by Irish workers and their families surrounding a now defunct mill. I hated saying goodbye. Though it was her home, it looked like a dangerous neighborhood for Grace, with traffic zooming by, oblivious to vagrant pets. I hope she's doing okay.

If only humans were as adaptable as dogs, they would see that all who ran before them are ancestors, that their neighborhood pack consists of sisters and brothers, and that even strays are siblings yearning for a lair. Then maybe they wouldn't yearn and long and whine so much for lost ancestral roots and missing family.

On Falling Trees

I get a kick out of watching David Letterman's "Stupid Human Tricks." I believe that among the stupidest human tricks are useless head games, like asking, "If a tree falls in the forest and no one (read: 'no *human*') is around, does it make a sound?" Humans are so narcissistic! As if the tree itself or God or other creatures wouldn't sense the reverberations of so great a loss!

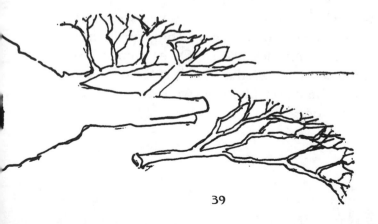

I know this firsthand, because several humans cut down some huge, old trees to build a house next door. When their trunks hit the ground, the earth trembled in response. My humans found me, shaking, underneath a desk on the other side of the house. They comforted me, believing me to be fearful for myself.

In reality, I was fearful for us all. I doubted the tree cutters thanked the tree for giving up its life, or asked for the tree's forgiveness, or even recognized that they had taken a life. That mother earth herself trembled indicated the great tragedy of this death, and I wondered what the anguished spirit of the tree might do in all of us who felt its great plunge to the ground.

Native Americans are among the few human packs who understand the awesome sacredness of nature, recognizing and respecting spirits in supposedly inanimate objects. Other humans seem oblivious to the truth that God is in the tree as much as in any human creature. No wonder they miss that God is in dogs, too.

On the Kindness
of Strangers

Like everyone, I can be skittish around strangers. But for the most part, I find others are more afraid of me than I am of them, and strangers are usually friendly and helpful. On the window-that-constantly-changes my humans watch things that make the opposite seem true. They just need a little dog sense to sniff out reality, though.

This was brought home to me on a trip to a pet store that allows me and other animals inside. I'm thrilled the instant we drive into the parking lot, and I can hardly wait to stroll the aisles sniffing the scents of other dogs and cats, as well as that strange scent that accompanies something that's new. I get to pick out a toy from shelves conveniently arranged at my height, while one of my humans loads a big bag and many cans of food into a shopping cart.

I pretend not to notice when a bag of pig ears is put in the basket, or a new bone, since my humans like to surprise me with these later. I am usually too excited to take one of the treats the human behind the counter gives me. Everyone I meet seems to love me, though they must love all animals, or they would not be there.

After one visit, we stopped somewhere for my human to run in and pick up some medicine that had already been ordered on the speaking-leash.* As usual, my human left the windows open for me, but then came back and closed them, saying something about a stranger poisoning dogs and being gone just a minute. There had been a story on the window-that-constantly-changes that morning about a serial dog killer in our city.

No sooner was my human gone than another human started hovering about, acting

---

* This is the Canine word for telephone. —Trans.

very excited, grabbing other humans who were passing by and pointing questioningly in my direction. I assumed that all this attention was because I looked so cute sitting behind the steering wheel— my usual perch when my human leaves me in the car. I grinned demurely (which is tough for dogs to do).

When my human came out, the other one seemed relieved. Evidently the stretched-leash-attitude* was caused by concern for my welfare, locked in a car with windows closed on a hot day. Explaining she had dogs, too, she offered to get me water, to my delight, and once again, I benefited from the kindness of strangers. That's why we in the dog world like to say, "A human is a dog's best friend."

The marrow of the story is that, while my human fretted unnecessarily about a stranger who might be a serial dog killer and risked my welfare to

---

* *Stretched-leash-attitude* is roughly the Canine equivalent of *stress*. The author considered using the German Shepherd word *angst* but decided against it because of a conviction that German shepherds have already been too influential in philosophical matters. —Trans.

protect me, I was graced with a stranger who was not about to let me come to harm.

Guess which one of us had a leg up on reality?

On Biting

Humans could learn a lot from dogs about biting. Not *how* to bite, but how to *limit* one's bite! We dogs can't throw our bites across the room or the globe by pulling a trigger or pushing a button, like humans can. That limits our bites' destructiveness, and we're also less likely to miss or mistake our target. And we get a mouthful of the damage we do to others, further reducing the likelihood of more bites than necessary to rout an opponent.

Though there are dogs, like humans, whose upbringing makes them more prone to attack, most of us bite only in self-defense or in defense of our pack. Unfortunately, humans belong to too many packs which they feel the need to defend. Sometimes I think they might end up biting *themselves*! Better for them to think of the earth as their lair and *all* humans as their pack—then they would have less to defend with their bites.

On Petting

Seems to me that humans demonstrate a certain disdain for their own bodies. In no instance is this more apparent than in the area of petting. When humans pet a dog, that's always good. But when humans pet each other, that is often problematic. In fact, petting sounds lurid to them when they mean petting between themselves, yet delightfully innocent when talking about animals.

This makes me feel sorry for humans. I could not survive if my humans didn't pat my head, scratch behind my ears, caress my neck, massage my back, play with my paws, and rub my tummy. There are, of course, areas that appropriate human discretion leaves untouched, but these areas I can attend to myself. Other dogs will also be attentive to parts of my anatomy that humans ignore.

When was the last time you rubbed your spouse's back? When was the last time you petted your child or your parent or your grandparent? When was the last time you nuzzled up to your brother and sister with warm affection?

All humans deserve to be touched, and so I do my bit to alleviate their isolation by licking the faces of everyone I meet. Sometimes there's a payoff—children's faces are particularly tasty because of all the sweet stuff smeared around their mouths, and I love the salty flavor of my human returning from a run. Yet these are not my main reasons. I'm just trying to show affection.

Now, it is true that humans are more devious than dogs. Sometimes they pet me just to get what they want—like nudging me into the bathtub for my shower. That's not exactly wrong, for I love my bath once it gets started and my human is

massaging the lather all over me and then rinsing me with spray. But petting another human to get something unwanted or unneeded by the receiving party—I believe that's wrong. That's what humans call pet-to-get.*

I think it's a shame that pet-to-get gets in the way of all petting between humans, however. I believe it's sad that teachers are afraid to pat their students' heads, that workers are afraid to hug one another in the workplace, that humans can't reach out and touch someone without fear of being misunderstood. (A small digression: I don't understand a communications company using "reach out and touch someone" as a slogan. You can't pet others by the

---

* This is the literal meaning of the Canine word for all forms of sexual exploitation. In contrast, the literal translation of the Canine word for lovemaking is *pet-to-give*. —Trans.

speaking-leash, not really. You can bark at them, growl, or whimper, but you can't lick their faces or lay your head on their laps.)

Humans need more touching, not less! The burden should not be placed entirely on the pet population! We're glad to do it but annoyed that humans don't shoulder their own responsibilities. Creatures were intended to touch. That's why we have bodies! On the window-that-constantly-changes I watched a documentary about a tribe of people who are *always* touching. That seems to be the natural state of humans. My humans sleep curled up together all night long—and they seem the happier for it. I know I'm the more content for sleeping next to them.

Perhaps if humans touched more, not in the pet-to-get sense, but out of pure affection and belonging, petting one another might not seem so titillating and might not be a cause for suspicion. Seems to me that much of the human preoccupation with breeding is really just a hunger for affection. Take it from a neutered dog—you can live without sex but *never* without affection. Instead of buying *Playboy* or *Playgirl*, humans should get a playdog!

On Leashes

Leashes are embarrassing. When I'm put on my leash it means I can't be trusted to behave, to be safe, to be good. I lose my sense of independence and personal responsibility. I lose my freedom.

It was a long while before I sensed that a leash was also embarrassing for my humans. They, too, feel humiliation as I tug on the leash, resisting them. They would prefer for me to behave, to be safe, to be good. They enjoy our walks most when there's mutual freedom. They no more want to be on the end of a leash than I do!

They are my lead dogs; that is, they are the ones whom I look to for guidance about where we're going, when we're stopping, when we're resting, when we're eating. They let me be the "lead dog" when I suggest it's time to play by dropping a ball in front of them, or coax them to be affectionate by nudging one of their hands with my nose onto my head for a pat and scratch, or remind them by my example how good it is just to "veg out" on the sofa.

Seems to me this is a good way to live. Wouldn't it be wonderful to live in a world without leashes, in which every creature behaved, where we took turns being lead dogs and no one was humiliated by being at either end of a leash? One of the things my humans learned about leashes in our training classes was not to pull against resistance—because we dogs (and most creatures) will not be persuaded by that method. Better to regain my attentiveness to follow their lead than for them to force their control.

This suggests to me something about the nature of God and those who represent God. God is the supreme Lead Dog, who persuades rather than coerces. And those who represent God best follow that lead by shepherding rather than bulldogging others. If *dogma* were true to its origin in the word *dog*, it would include this lesson learned from dogs: that none of us is to pull against resistance by forcing our beliefs or our spiritual path on others. Instead, being dogmatic has simply become another form of leashing and muzzling.

(By the way, I don't find those bumper stickers that read "MY KARMA JUST RAN OVER YOUR DOGMA" the least bit funny.)

On Muzzles

Since I just alluded to muzzles, I sensed the need to comment on them. There are times when a muzzle is a good thing and times when it is not. When getting my nails clipped, I need to be muzzled because I involuntarily snap at those attempting to do me (and them) the favor. But if I were muzzled all the time, I wouldn't be able to cool myself off by panting, let alone eat, drink, or defend our lair.

It's true that some humans need to muzzle themselves occasionally. They defensively snap at those trying to help them, too. But if they were muzzled all the time, their temperature would rise in anger, not to mention that they would go hungry, get dehydrated, and be rendered unable to defend themselves and others.

Humans have a bigger den to defend than I do: they have a global lair that they must watchdog to make sure fellow humans aren't maltreated or allowed to go hungry. That might require barking or snapping to keep at bay those who bark and snap at those unable to defend themselves. Unfortunately, most of the barking and snapping I witness among humans (especially on the window-that-constantly-changes) should be muzzled, or saved for the really vicious humans in defense of others.

On Being
Close to the Ground

Being close to the ground means I can easily "stop to smell the roses," a rather tired human cliché I *still* hear on the window-that-constantly-changes. (I guess this indicates that things don't change as much as is supposed.) Truth is, I can easily smell all kinds of things, which I do, from cats to underground bugs, and from food spills to big canned food.* Humans differentiate between "good" and "bad" smells more than I do. All odors have something to tell me, though not so much as they told the French author Proust. (I added the bit about Proust so you would know me to be a well-bred dog, albeit a mixed one.)

I can smell shoes and know if my humans have been to the park without me. At the park, my nose quickly leads me to where picnickers have been, or where dogs have left their scents. I am particularly

---

* What dogs call garbage cans. —Trans.

fond of the smell of piles of leaves. Walking around the block, I almost get lightheaded snorting so many different aromas on sidewalks, trees, bushes, and lawns. In the house, I sleep more easily in places where my scent and my humans' scents are found.

And I get excited sniffing other dogs in places that humans generally find distasteful.

My human translator looks at me doubtfully as I add that I can also smell fear, lust, anger, and danger. But I believe that bodies generate different smells given the occasion. Certainly my humans smell different when they're making love than when they're arguing. I know to stay off the bed in the first case; and to stay under the coffee table in the second.

On Dogs
in Scripture

I have been told by some (whose motives* I seriously question) that dogs are not positively portrayed in the scriptures of various religions. We are associated with depravity, paganism, heresy, enemies, and the lowest of the low. We are described as licking up blood or returning to our own vomit. Jesus said not to give us what's holy, but agreed, at least, that we had a right to eat the crumbs that fall from our master's table.

This last reference must serve as the can-opener** to reveal God's intentions with regard to dogs. Canine prejudice abounded when most religious canons were written. Surely this admittedly fleeting reference to our right to whatever falls from our masters' tables gives dogs new status in

---

* The literal translation from the Canine is *bones-in-hiding*. —Trans.

** Here the word is used as *hermeneutic,* or *method of interpretation*. —Trans.

scriptural dogma. Only those who don't like us would use the other scriptures against us.

And, reading scriptures as a whole, it's clear that God is usually on the side of the underdog, and there's nothing more "under" than us dogs!

On Resting

One of the great differences I notice (and I must admit, enjoy) between my lifestyle and that of my humans is the attitude toward rest. I am praised for it, humans are criticized for it. My humans seem pleased that I sleep so much. Less is demanded of them, and they have time to tend to their own lives. Indeed, as I lie dozing in various positions, I often hear comments like: "Oh, isn't that cute?" "Quick, get the camera!" "Puppy's sleepy."

In contrast, when one of my humans is sleeping too long or at the wrong time of day, the other might say things like: "Aren't you up yet?" "Don't you have something to do?" "You're just being lazy!" The tone of voice used is like what I hear if I get into the trash.

I believe this is an area in which humans have much to learn from dogs. In one of their theologies, after all, it is said that even God rested a full day after six days of creation! It seems to me that if only humans rested more, they wouldn't be so snarly, anxious, and high-strung. If they took a series of short naps during the day, or just curled up occasionally for a few minutes and did no work, whatever they did would be far more effective and enjoyable. Indeed, I am pleased to say that I have served as a lead dog for my humans as they often join me for a dog nap.

Generally, humans tend to save up their sleep for nighttime. But even then they sometimes appear to be working in their sleep. Sporadically I watch them in the middle of the night, their eyes closed but faces scrunched up in nocturnal problem-solving. Occasionally they wake me with their mumblings and, less often, yelps. The other night one of my humans barked, "Summer jobs! Summer jobs! There are still summer jobs!" Another time, one of them groaned in terror, "No, don't let them get me!" But usually, they just say boring things like: "No, let's have the meeting here." "This isn't done right." "Yes, we'll have to . . ." I'm training them to let go of all their troubles in one giant exhale of breath when they're ready to sleep at night.

I also dream when I sleep, but my dreaming is an extension of my pleasurable life: I'm running in the park, chasing squirrels, or riding in the window-that-moves* with my head stuck out in the breeze.

My poor humans seem to dream more about problems than pleasure, and I believe that's because, from the time they're puppies, they're taught an inhumane attitude toward real rest. It's as if they are trained, "If you truly let go, you're not being responsible." Saint Augustine testified to the need for absolute rest when he wrote, "My soul is restless, until it rest in thee, O God." Humans take their activities so seriously, they can't seem to let them go even at the end of their walks.**

As for me, I find I'm much more attentive to catching a ball or chasing a frisbee if I stop thinking about it when I'm not doing it. It's a Zen thing.

---

* The usual Canine word for car literally means *window-that-moves*. An alternative but colloquial term for car is *window-that-blows-in-my-face*. —Trans.

** Here *walk* is the Canine equivalent for *day*. Apparently dogs think that when humans go off to work each day, even in their cars, they're going for an extended walk or run. Dogs can't understand why humans go on these walks or runs independently, rather than in a pack. Car pools, therefore, make more sense to them. —Trans.

On Eating
from Sacks

My humans frequently remark about how quickly I eat. They usually feed me from a large sack in the pantry. Before they close the sack I'm almost finished eating. But I've noticed they eat almost as fast when they eat from sacks. In fact, they call it "fast food."

In the evenings, when I get canned food mixed in with the bagged food, I wait for the wet meat to be put atop the dry nuggets before I dive in. It's worth waiting to taste the mix of flavors. My humans also slow down to eat when they prepare their meals. Then they seem to have all the time in the world, especially when they have guests. I sense they enjoy eating then, just as I slow down to relish chewing my bone or devouring a pig's ear.

There's something about waiting to eat, taking time for it to be prepared, that adds savor to the flavor.

On Veterinarians

There is something out of balance about the fact that my human readily takes me to the vet for my annual checkups and occasional problems, yet hesitates to go to the doctor. My human even has medical insurance, something I don't have, and yet worries* about the high cost of medical care for humans.

My vet takes as much time and as much care and is as kind as my human's doctor, yet charges a fraction of the cost. I cannot help but wonder—indeed, I must suppose—that the low cost of routine medical care for animals reflects an undervaluation of our worth. But I can't quite conclude that the high cost of routine medical care for humans reflects a comparative overvaluation of human worth. I've seen too much undervaluation of human life on the window-that-constantly-changes to believe that. I be-

---

* There is almost no Canine equivalent for *worries*. The closest idiom, and the one Calvin uses here, is *chews-up-the-rug*. —Trans.

lieve rather that the human fear of debilitation, loss, and death gets exploited by doctors and insurance* companies.

I love the existentialism inherent in being a dog. I live for the moment. I may bury a bone for later consumption, but I do not anticipate illness or death, let alone worry about it. I wonder in smells and sights and sounds here before me. When death comes I will wonder in the smells and sights and

---

* *Insurance* is a difficult concept for dogs to comprehend. Their closest experience of it is *burying bones,* which is the phrase Calvin uses here. —Trans.

sounds of it too. If I follow the lead of others of my kind, I will likely choose to be by myself and away from the pack as that time approaches, just as a Hindu might dedicate himself or herself to an ascetic life of meditation toward the end of life.

A human might call my attitude the height of denial. But in reality, it's the height of innocence.

On Randomness and Spontaneity

At first my humans very much disliked it when I played croquet with them, catching those balls as I've been taught to catch others. They'd tie me up or hold me back, especially when they had invited guests to play. But eventually they decided to accept my participation, and they renamed the game "Calvinball," after the game of some comic strip character who constantly changed the rules of a game as he went. I don't really like this, since I'm playing by the rules they taught me (they throw a ball and I pick it up in my mouth), and I'm afraid people will think I'm named for a character from the comics rather than the theologian from which both our names are taken.

But I do like the fact that, by incorporating my playfulness into the game, my humans have (in a small way) accepted the random nature of the universe. Not everything can go according to plan, not everything happens within the rules. They laugh

more when I play with them, and their competition is less fierce. When I pick up a ball, its owner coaxes me to drop it advantageously. When I don't, the owner whines and the other yips happily. They also attempt to distract me by throwing my own ball. I add a lot to the game, and we all get much more aerobic activity.

I believe that opening ourselves up to spontaneity welcomes serendipity, when grace or joy or love comes unexpectedly. Mystical experiences are serendipitous in nature anyway, no matter how accomplished one becomes at spiritual obedience school.

On Watchfulness

If attentiveness is the can-opener* to understanding both creatures and Creator, watchfulness
is the can-opener to appreciating life itself. During
my waking hours, I keep watch, looking for opportunities to play, connect with others, eat, and defend
my turf when necessary. Watchfulness is not something you simply do with your eyes. It is done with
every available sense. So, even in sleep, I may hear
my human's key in the door or an intruder's step on
the porch, smell the opening of a can of dog food or
the scent of meat unpackaged for the grill.

---

* There is no way to render in human language the reveren-
tial connotation that the Canine language gives to *can-opener*.
It's best to think of it as the source of life itself, considering its
use to open cans of dog food. But it suggests more than mere
survival; it also inculcates the merriment that *corkscrew* or *bottle
opener* implies for humans. Remember, canned dog food is more
of a gourmet treat than the usual dry dog food that comes in
mere sacks. —Trans.

The latter got me into trouble when I was a puppy and taught me that watchfulness does not necessarily mean acting on impulse. My human had set out two steaks on the kitchen counter, then went outside to light the grill. In a flash, I downed one steak and was discovered with the other on the floor. The one I ate I hadn't taken the time to savor. This is, I must admit, an indelicate doggie trait. Our genes learned long ago to eat on the run.

Ostensibly for my health, though I suspect actually in retribution, I was given the salt treatment—a teaspoonful of salt to make me regurgitate the steak. I felt a twinge of shame that only one bite mark was on the filet mignon. I never did that again, though I must admit I've never been given the opportunity either.

Whereas the application may not always be appropriate, I still believe in the principle behind my action. Seizing the moment (*carpe diem*, or *seizing the day*, is too large a bite even for me) or seizing an opportunity to enjoy the gifts of life is a good way to live. I never refuse a pat on the head, a treat, a walk in the park, a ride in the car, an opportunity to doze on the floor. Now, there are times when I don't eat my dish of food right away, and, of course, I don't constantly chew on my bone, but knowing both are there offers me a pleasurable content.

I believe the stretched-leash-attitude of my humans largely comes from a disability to sniff out the opportunities for pleasure even within the confines of their lair, yard, or routine.

Canine watchfulness combines both Zen attentiveness to the present and Christian anticipation of the future kingdom of God.

On the
Edible Complex

My humans complain that I've never met food I didn't like. This is not an eating disorder, for it's in my nature to scavenge whatever edible delectables I can find, especially now that they've put me on a diet because I was getting a bit paunchy. It's true that I sniff and taste all kinds of things, especially at the park, causing them to scrunch their faces in disgust or reach in my mouth to retrieve whatever I've bolted lest I choke or get sick.

I notice this is not just a canine thing, but a human thing as well, though humans express it differently. One of my humans buys more clothes than can be worn and the other buys more books than there's time to read. On the window-that-constantly-changes I watch humans encouraged in and even rewarded for their edible complex through commercials, game shows, lottery drawings, and an entire cable channel devoted to this dangerous instinct.

I believe that humans need to be more attentive to their Higher Power scrunching a face with disgust, wanting to prevent them from choking or getting sick. Providentially, for the worst addictions, there is obedience school for humans where they learn Twelve Steps to restrain their impulses. In my own training program, I was taught a special version of the Serenity Prayer:

God grant me the serenity
To surrender the things I cannot eat,
And swallow the things I can,
And the sense to know the difference.

On God

God's a mother dog, the supreme Lead Dog. Both my translator and my editor have discouraged me from reclaiming the proper word for "mother dog," because humans use it as a curse. Just because humans have made it a derogatory term doesn't mean we dogs use it that way. Consider the term *God* itself as another example of how often a sacred and wholesome word gets used as profanity. Terms about the wonders of petting get misused as curses, too.

God's a mother dog who births us and then offers a teat for everyone to suckle on. We are weaned, sure enough, but at rough times in our lives or at the end of our lives, the teat reappears to nurture and sustain us. God's warm belly is the best place to rest in peace, in life and in death.

Inasmuch as I was separated from my own mother shortly after I was weaned, this metaphor for God has kept me going. Hidden within me and I suspect within every creature, there is a whimper of longing to return to Mother God.

Now it is also true that many creatures had a "mad dog" for a mother, by whom they were bitten or snapped at or abandoned. It's more difficult for them to identify with God as wonderfully kind when their mother treated them badly or with indifference. Others have been mistakenly *taught* that God is a mad dog, ready to growl or bite them at the slightest provocation. I do not believe that a "mad dog" God is worthy of our attentiveness.

Sometimes the teachers of a mad dog God are well-intentioned, simply not knowing any better. They have missed the gracious nature of God just as my human missed the gracious nature of dogs when bitten by Freckles as a child. But sometimes these teachers are mean-spirited, seemingly untrainable by God's gracious love. Perhaps they unleash their *hubris*—the arrogant pride that is one of the seven deadly human sins—on others, believing only they themselves are worthy of God's love.

Now, of course, God does growl from time to time, when we engage in behavior that's inappropriate, like biting one another or fouling our own nest or demanding a teat too much for God's comfort, our own independence, and fairness to others. But God doesn't bite her own puppies. God is a kind Dog who puts up with a lot, always welcomes us to her bosom, and defends us to the death against all comers.

I am very proud to call myself a son of that kind of [mother dog].*

---

* Translator's substitution.

On Fleas

You are always going to have to deal with fleas. You can lessen their prevalence, but life is always going to present you with bites, itches, and irritations. The best thing to do is cope with them as best you can, and accept help when offered.

I have often wondered why a good God would allow or ordain the existence of fleas. I have wondered if their presence is some kind of test of the canine spirit. On the other paw, fleas may serve as a physical blessing in disguise. Having fleas has kept me limber, as I've had to stretch to bite at them or contort my body to scratch at them. Maybe the spiritual benefit is similar.

Fleas have kept me from fully embracing the principles of the Jains, a Hindu sect which worries so much about taking life that some wear protective masks to avoid unintentionally killing microbes. But it does make me wonder about reincarnation. What if dogs and fleas are eternally sentenced to a kind of revolving karmic reincarnation where fleas become dogs and dogs become fleas? Dogs pay for their murders by becoming those they kill; and fleas pay for their torture by becoming the tortured. Enlightenment or nirvana would mean deliverance from the cycle.

In the meantime, I'm grateful that flea spray is a legal weapon and that nobody who champions reproductive rights or condemns contraception as sin has challenged flea pills that keep them from reproducing.

On Death
and Resurrection

As I wrote earlier, every dog, almost by defini-
tion, is essentially an existentialist. We live for the
moment. Time is a human construct.*

So death is difficult for us to grasp. And death is
something that happens to others, not to us. Humans understand and share this belief, but for them
it's denial, whereas for us it's reality.

One of my humans goes off after we wake up
in the morning and does not return until our final
feeding. The other stays and sits, punching but-
tons of a window-that-spits-up-paper.** On occasion this human goes away for many feedings,

---

* In this, as well as throughout the book, I've included "time
words" to facilitate human readers' understanding. But words
referencing time are not in a dog's vocabulary. For example, in
this reflection, I have added words like *after*, *until*, *before*, *when*,
and *since*. To whatever degree that dogs mark time, it's done by
number of feedings, naps, and walks. —Trans.
** Canine for computer. —Trans.

naps, and walks, and I can tell departure is imminent long before the bag is packed. At night I snuggle closer.

Death, to me, is their absence. That's why I wag my tail so heartily when I see them again, for their presence is resurrection. These constant resurrections prevent me from thinking that any death is permanent.

Since I started writing my philosophy, two things have happened. First, our neighbors Wilson and Kensey moved to a new lair, apparently far away. Through my window, I kept watching for them outside their den across the street. And, at the park, whenever I saw a human puppy, I ran to lick its face, thinking it might be Wilson. Then Wilson appeared out of nowhere for a visit, confirming my belief in life beyond what I can see. This time he was bigger, having turned twenty-one in dog years (three in human years), and I wondered if resurrection makes one bigger each time.

The other thing that's happened is that Buster, the old dog down the street, died. For many walks past his house I could still smell his scent and wanted to stop and visit. Gradually his scent faded, but I nonetheless watch for him behind his gate. I know that I will see him and play with him once more. Maybe next time.

On Leaving
Your Mark

We all want to leave our scent so others will know we've passed this way. It's another way of claiming our territory: far more subtle than barking, and far sexier, too. And, as much as we would like our mark to be permanent, leaving it requires daily repetition. Scents fade, rains wash away our markings, others leave their scent on top of ours, and ours blends in with all the others.

We would like our scent to be unique and eternal. But perhaps more important, we would like our markings to be acknowledged and appreciated—at least by someone who will be attracted by our scent, someone who will roll around in it delightedly, someone who may offer us momentary intimacy and ecstasy. But beyond that moment, we again yearn to leave a distinctive mark forever on our world.

This is when I find my ancestors instructive, the dogs who went before me in the lives of my humans.

Though I've never met them, I know them through the love of the very humans who love me. I know them as unique personalities that helped shape the human responses I presently enjoy. If their scent is not present anymore in the world, a sense of them is in the heart of my humans whose love was enlarged enough by their mark to welcome me into this world and to love me better than they were able to love my ancestors.

I believe this is how we leave our unique and eternal mark on the world—making a better lair for those who follow.

Epilogue:
On Writing Philosophy

I've worked like a dog on this book—that is to say, I've taken it one reflection at a time, spaced out with plenty of play, naps, meals, treats, petting, licking, and simple watching out my window. I believe that's the best way to offer bones that are any good to the world.

My hope is that, by following the same routine, you will come up with your own philosophy of life that keeps you on your walk and helps others on theirs. Avoid that misnamed "dog-eat-dog" world (after all, *we're* not cannibals) and drool over a dog-sniff-dog world in which we smell one another's delicious scents, see the wonder of all creation, dig out a safe lair for all (especially puppies), perk up our ears at worthy lead dogs, take opportunities to rest and play and nest, and sense the presence of our Mother Dog watching over all of us.

Then together, as one pack, we can sniff out life's buried treats.

Treats

Doggie treats all around for the humans at Westminster John Knox Press who made this book pawsable. They've all been such good boys and good girls! Managing Editor Stephanie Egnotovich (Why do humans have such long names?) encouraged my translator to pursue the publication of my thoughts as only a dog lover could. Jim Kelley has captured my endearing personality in his illustrations. Jennifer Cox designed a book that even I could devour. Amy Brack helped my translator clarify the English version of my Canine as copyeditor. Annie McClure is getting the word out about my book so I can make a bundle of doggie treats. And lots of humans have assisted them and still others will be printing, marketing, distributing, selling, and, most importantly—*buying and reading this book! Good* humans! *Good* humans! Last but not least, I want to thank my humans for their support (including the translation), as well as the Lead Dog who inspires us all along our spiritual runs.

Calvin